Towns Of Puerto Rico

CONTENTS

3	Adjuntas
5	Aguada
7	Aguas Buenas
9	Arecibo
11	Barceloneta
13	Cabo Rojo
15	Canovanas
17	Ceiba
19	Corozal
21	Fajardo
23	Guanica
25	Guaynabo
27	Humacao
29	Isabela

31	Lajas
33	Lares
35	Mayaguez
37	Naranjito
39	Ponce
41	Rincon
43	San German
45	San Juan
47	San Juan 2
49	San Juan 3
51	San Juan 4
53	San Sebastian
55	Utuado
57	Vieques
59	Yauco

Towns Of Puerto Rico

Towns Of Puerto Rico

Towns Of Puerto Rico

Towns Of Puerto Rico

Towns Of Puerto Rico

Towns Of Puerto Rico

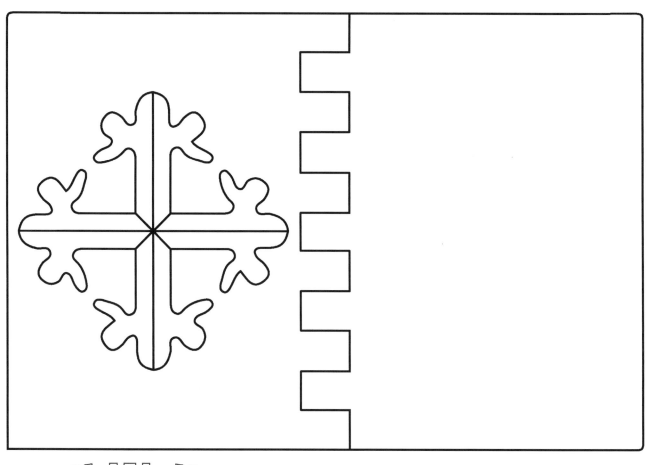

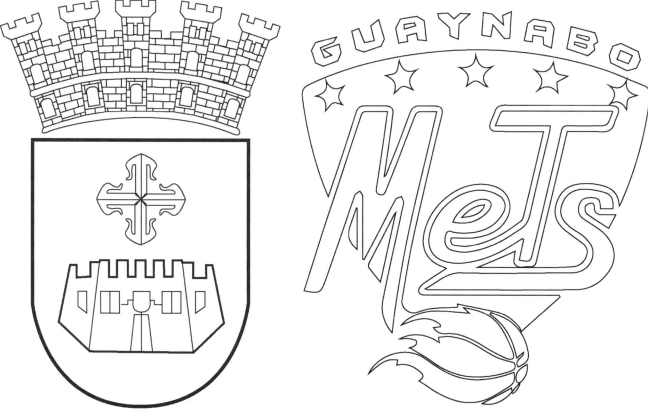

Towns Of Puerto Rico

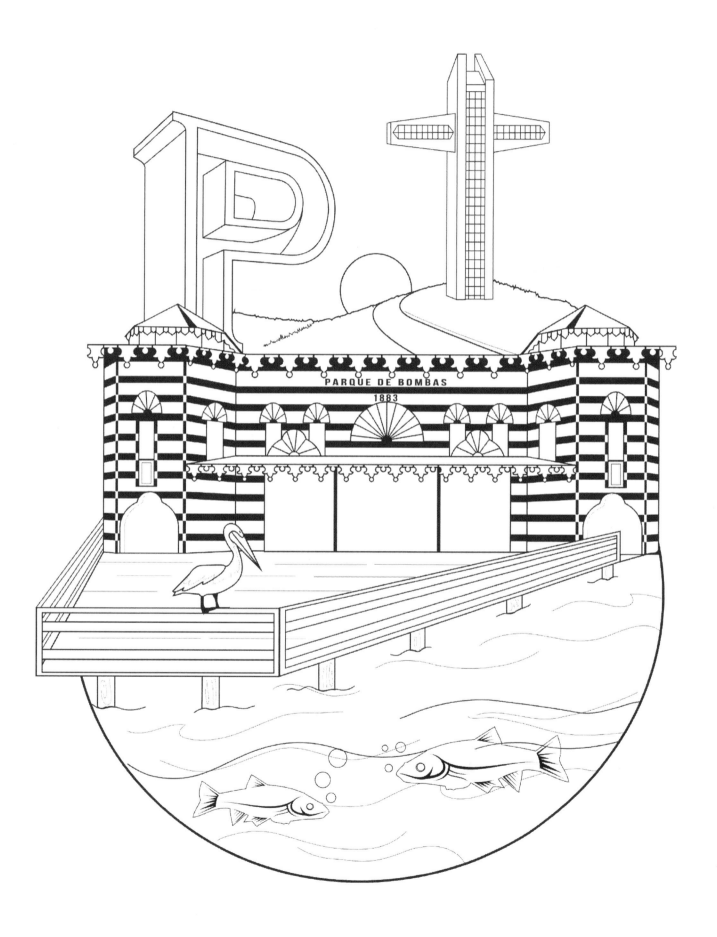

Towns Of Puerto Rico

Towns Of Puerto Rico

Towns Of Puerto Rico

Towns Of Puerto Rico

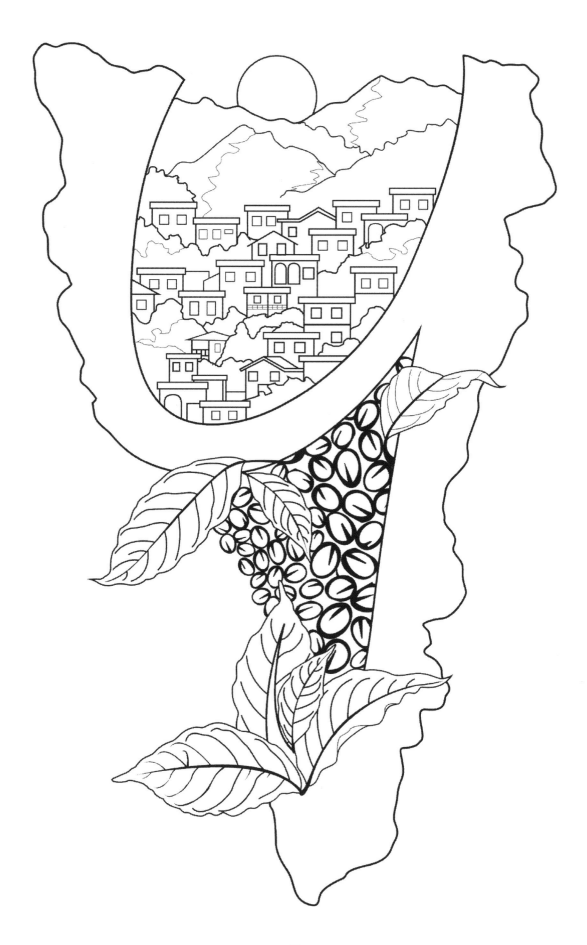

ABOUT THE CREATION OF THIS BOOK

This book is a project produced by Puerto Rico Presenta (http://puertoricopresenta.com) . Adult coloring is a great activity that promotes relaxation, we saw the need to bring puertorican themes to the scene. The creation effort was led by Alfredo Alvarez. Illustrations were made by a great team of illustrators from the Island. Including Rafael Pagan, Victoria Cano, Xavier Ocasio, Alexander Damiani and Carlos Fernandez.

Feel free to contact us at: alfredo.e.alvarez@gmail.com

Made in the USA
Middletown, DE
02 October 2018